The Sorry History of Fast Food

Paul Sutton

Open House Editions

Published by Open House Editions
an imprint of Leafe Press
www.leafepress.com

Acknowledgements:

Parts of this sequence first appeared in Stride and International Times. Many
thanks to their editors.

A. Political Property

I.

Of course haunting is true,
wherever it comes from. Perhaps
one-in-ten homes are memory traps.

I mean those gravel-rendered
semis of the London suburbs.
Desolation in the heat or rain.

Almost an old man, in the sickly
quiet of hedges behind plane trees.
I was followed back once.

Nothing to worry you now.
A man of string, fingers
clutching dead mice.

II.

When I watch property programmes,
I'm astounded that places I shuddered
from as slums, now sell for millions.
Actually, the worst glowered down on
Euston Road, where Capital Radio went.
I saw it from the old hospital, wondering
'Who lives behind those perforated curtains?'
and beneath the archway was a grim ravine.

The areas around old stations did it best.
That's why regeneration of King's Cross,
or even worse Paddington, was such a loss.
Remember those Italian cafes, which served

spaghetti to toothy war brides and cascading
knickerbocker glories to girls clutching dolls?
We knew the coffee was Thames mud and
loved it all the more for being so bad.

There's no doubt we were filthier then
and our teeth lurked like mustard gas.
What's really changed though are smells;
shops then — cardboard and the saturated
expected aroma of an old man's crotch.
London was wonderful in soot and dust,
even the rain smelt like bomb damage and
stations of cigarettes which can't be captured.

On warm evenings, I go back to school for a
production. That vast sun through plate glass,
in a summer of total heat. Guessing there was
any government, happy or just funding it, in
the sure assumption of Garden City utopia —
they felt class had finished —
it hadn't of course, although
for children it could be true.

III.

A drowned baby, bare
feet stand on its back.

Men in top-hats decapitated, masked
activists kick their heads into the sea.

(Stop any agreement, daemon
with a frozen logic of virtue.)

Just nothing for defying ochlocracy:
a mass rally screaming its sanctimony.

Projected into my home and body.
I can't complain though.

The sun still shines, so the garden
shows pure green in warming blue.

I can masturbate at leisure
now frozen food is available.

Not from the sky, but some movement
in the pine trees has me unconcerned.

B. A History of Heatwaves

It started in 1976. I never realised
why English people feared the sun.

That green of suffocation. Cycling
a wooded lane, shadows glimpsed
in a river. Seen too near, as ghosts.

Intoxication, of elderflower and wild,
sharp roots. Anyone can find the centre
in hidden woods and no one goes there.

C. My Boy Jack

I.

My first visit to the Jack the Ripper
conference; in a shivery suit, shiny
yet pasty faced. I could have been
some pallid clerk, a spring-heeled
escapee from the Abyss.

How naïve not to realise
that others do the same;
proposing an ancestor
as the latest suspect.

My great-uncle's disgraceful papers.

Some motorway service station.

(Impossible not to love them,
their invocation of oblivion;
a linear fast-food heaven.

My record was five hours
spent eating and defecating.)

Underneath an abandoned mop.
His old journal, sealed in pig fat.

II.

(from *The Journal of Mutatis Mutandis*)

Fuck me, I'm tired.

Spent.

Like a ginger beer bottle, exploding at some daft street fair.

Now my sons, look at that photograph of me in whiskers.

My ramrod cock hidden.

An iron stare.

Clearly a cunt — and you only know the half.

Too easy avoiding the 'rozzers'.

I used an electric moped — though scarcely invented then —
working as a pizza delivery boy.

No one suspected a thing!

My blood-spotted uniform
taken as some new topping.

The area was gentrifying
from days of plague dogs
and leper chips.

Opportunities overflowing.

Why these immigrants —
to chronicle the rain?

I now explain my actions in terms of diversification.
Providing a safe environment, where creative types
can network and rediscover squalor — at a distance.

III.

"Preposterous.

Monstrous.

Tedious."

(A letter, from the Psychogeographic Poets.)

"Sinclairian rehash! Another rip-off
 bike-seat sniffer on Saucy Jack riff."

Many poets moved to Spitalfields.
Drinking wheatbeer where his
'Unfortunates' slugged gin.

Leylines, ranting tracts,
recycled toe rags from
forgotten antiquarians.

Ridiculous — our true country
is pure retail park, B & Q.

D. My work on TripAdvisor

God knows why Wetherspoons is sneered at.
It's the equivalent of a Victorian chophouse.

More genuine than identikit gastropubs —
infinite goatees, gorging on brick or slate.

Let's admit to it, the English
have always scoffed anything.

I can trace my history
through such disasters.

Did you try Elizabethan
"offal and hoof quickbits"
on the dizzy South Bank?

Or the "chipped potatoes"
on Whitechapel Road?

Boiled cabbage greens,
the grease on the cobbles,
a trudge to the next house.

It wasn't much.

E. Street Chicken

I am now convinced that my old Cambridge tutor — Maxwell Otto Cornelius — was Jack the Ripper.

Item 1:

A sperm-stained copy of Newton's *Principia*.

Purloined from Trinity library,
endpapers removed,
passages redacted.

Repetitive marginalia:

"Exterminate the brutes!"

Item 2:

A complex amalgam of hieroglyphs, pentagrams, ostrich feathers and fast-food napkins.

Specific links to Poussin's *A Dance to the Music of Time* — erroneous Latin motto, wrongly attributed to George Formby.

Item 3:

Space prohibits a fuller explanation of my methods.

Viz:

DNA testing on seagull carcass remains, with cross-referencing to filial genomes and mutant Subway chicken wraps, matches 92% hypochondriacal material to a towering Latvian lady, now working in Nando's.

Cornelius obsessed with her — proposing marriage.

Rejection spawning incipient misogyny and insanity.

A fast train to King's Cross — then underground to Aldgate East.

I myself espied him
in a Brick Lane tandoori;
ruddy stains on fingers and wrists.

Engaged in diversionary assault on poppadoms —
numerous lurid dips — one of bright carnelian red.

Perfect trace element match re.
ink in *Dear Boss* letter.

F. Human once

Where is the pity
in any of this?

Easy to objectify,
in black and white.

No access to their
memories: smiles
as a child of joy;
dad thowing them
in the air and then
held secure.

G. Jupiter

Holst's giddy joy,
a pride, history and triumph —
you to play it, again, again,
in green English fields —
assurance, love, trust.

It's now I need to write of it;
in some tone to match
old feelings with words.

Cut away this soggy and anxious fog.
Somewhere over the western waves
return to shade, a sapphire light,
and melodies by river meadows,
not caring when lost.

Why any shame in writing about this?
It's only a sound,
pure cadence;
just words.

H. Rituals around the dead

They show their videos:

Last meals; threats; landscapes; words.
Broadcast into loved ones' dreams —
a jolt, then we long for the repeat.

On a coast of ruined industry.

People who never see
far-distant mountains
or feel pine-cool air.

The bodies caried into parched fields.

To long mangled and dead trees,
then dissected in intricate ways —
from texts by 19th-century maniacs.

It doesn't matter now; they're 'passed'.

But the food eaten greedily
at these Saturnalian rituals?
It is of the worst kind.

The heat is all I recall.

In suffocating
nights under a
flickering sky.

Wet of sweat-
tangled dreams,
creeper bound.

Tarred, fly-devoured.
Driven near dawn into
yellow-throned swamp.

I. The Room

There is a room where everyone goes.
I don't mean death, or anything close.

The body drags around a mind,
then one day leaves it behind.

Long lost as animals;
believing in thoughts,

worshipping identical
sensations. Radiation

just whacks us forever.
And only pity matters.

www.ingramcontent.com/pod-product-compliance
Lightning Source LLC
LaVergne TN
LVHW090417090426
835511LV00042B/544